Alcoholism

About the pamphlet
Alcoholism: A Merry-Go-Round Named Denial depicts the cycle of alcoholism and illustrates its effects on the alcoholic, family members, and others who figure in the alcoholic's life. The pamphlet discusses the dynamics that shape how the alcoholic and family members respond to the problem and to each other, and it offers suggestions on how to get off the merry-go-round.

About the author
The Reverend Joseph L. Kellermann was a retired Episcopal priest who spent years helping families cope with the problem of alcoholism. He was the founder and former executive director of the Charlotte (North Carolina) Council on Alcoholism and received the 1991 Humanitarian Award from the National Council on Alcoholism and Drug Dependence.

Hazelden Classics for Intervention

Alcoholism
A Merry-Go-Round Named Denial

Revised Edition

Joseph L. Kellermann

HAZELDEN

Hazelden
Center City, Minnesota 55012-0176

1-800-328-9000
1-651-213-4590 (Fax)
www.hazelden.org

ISBN: 978-0-89486-022-5

Any stories or case studies used in this material are composites of many individuals. Names and details have been changed to protect identities.

Cover and interior design by David Spohn
Typesetting by Tursso Companies

INTRODUCTION

Alcoholism is a human drama, oftentimes tragic, that is played out in three repeated acts by four or more persons. As with many human problems, alcoholism doesn't develop or maintain itself in isolation. One person drinks inappropriately, and others react to the drinking and its consequences. The drinker responds to the reaction and drinks again. This sets up a merry-go-round of accusation, denial, and counterdenial that is called alcoholism. In order to understand how alcoholism develops and maintains itself, we must view the illness as if we were sitting in a theater watching a play, and we must observe carefully the roles of all the actors in the drama.

As the play begins, we see the alcoholic standing front and center as the subject of this act, while all other actors are the objects of the alcoholic's action. Alcoholics can be male or female and represent a wide range of ages and stations in life. They display a variety of personalities, behaviors, capabilities, and interests. The primary thing that sets them apart is their addiction and related behavior characteristics.

Alcoholics learn by chance or experimentation that alcohol use has profound, psychologically beneficial effects on them, in that alcohol temporarily dissolves anxiety, reduces tension, removes loneliness, and appears to solve problems. If a situation becomes unpleasant or even unbearable, there is the conscious or unconscious knowledge that a few drinks will provide instant relief. For alcoholics, this is a psychological blessing, and regardless of the many and varied curses it may create, the use of this substance becomes the most important thing in their lives because of its enormous immediate benefits.

The personality characteristics ascribed to the actors in this drama should be considered representative but not inflexible, since people cope with stress in different ways. The following is only one example of how this drama might play out.

1

ACT 1

The play opens with the alcoholic, or addict, standing center stage, loudly asserting his or her independence and competence (especially as it relates to family) to another actor who has appeared on stage.

It is obvious to the viewer that there is little communication between these two people, since the conversation is more like a one-way street than an exchange of viewpoints and opinions. The alcoholic appears to hear nothing that is said about his or her drinking. The other person seems to be confused, taking one verbal position in the beginning and backing off later. The words exchanged are of little or no importance to what is happening. This is why it is necessary to watch the play as it unfolds in order to understand the nature of alcoholism. To observe the alcoholic alone, to read a clinical evaluation, and to listen to the woes of family and friends are only small pieces of the drama. The key word in this drama is *denial*, for there is constant contradiction between what is happening and what is being said by all the actors in the play. If the play were being done in pantomime, it would be far less confusing.

Early in the first act, a situation arises that results in the alcoholic drinking. When the alcoholic begins to drink, the audience sees that he or she drinks hard and fast, ingesting alcohol in large amounts. This person may drink openly but is more apt to conceal the amount consumed by drinking offstage and rarely in the presence of other cast members. This is a major aspect of denial—concealing the amount consumed. If the alcoholic were not conscious of overdrinking, there would be no need to conceal the amount, time, place, or circumstances of drinking. The alcoholic denies drinking excessively but in reality drinks more than the social norm and more frequently than others. Alcohol means more to the alcoholic than it does to other people.

Excessive drinking is not a matter of choice for the alcoholic, it is a necessity. The repeated denial by concealment indicates the tremendous importance of alcohol's psychological effects for the drinker, and after the alcoholic has a few drinks, the audience witnesses another change in him or her. Alcohol gives this person a sense of competence, well-being, and self-sufficiency. It seems to put the alcoholic on top of the world, and it gives him or her a sense of superiority. The alcoholic is now right, and all others are wrong, if there is a difference of opinion or if anyone voices objections to the drinking or inappropriate behavior. Of course, there is no one particular act or deed that all alcoholics perform while intoxicated, but there is a continuing revelation of irrational, irresponsible, antisocial, and, at times, deviant or criminal behavior. Driving a vehicle under the influence is a common example of a combination of these behaviors.

As the drinking continues, the alcoholic creates a crisis and ends up in trouble. Again, there is an infinite variation in how this is done, but the basic movement in act 1 is always the same. Alcoholics most often attempt to conceal their dependency by denying it; they drink in order to feel superindependent, and as the drinking continues, they end up in a mess. Paradoxically, they then must depend on others to protect them from or to remove the consequences of the mess they have created. Often when they find themselves in a mess—whether it be of a mild, antisocial, or even criminal nature—they will simply wait for something to happen. They may ignore it, walk or run away from it, or cry for someone to get them out of it. Most important, they are now painfully aware that they are totally dependent on others.

Act 1 begins with the star of the drama, the alcoholic, declaring his or her independence. As the curtain closes on the act, we see the star, who earlier claimed complete independence, in a mess created by his or her own drinking behavior. Alcohol, which in the beginning gave the alcoholic a sense of superiority, independence, and ultimate well-being, has stripped him or her of the costume of independence and superiority. We now see the alcoholic as being much like a helpless, dependent child.

ACT 2

In act 2, our star, the alcoholic, becomes completely passive—the "object" of the other characters who appear in this act.

The Enabler

The first person to appear on stage in response to the alcoholic's dilemma is one we will call the Enabler, a guilt-laden, overly responsible individual whose own anxiety and sense of guilt will not let him or her endure the predicament of the friend or loved one, the alcoholic. This person sets up a "rescue mission" to save the alcoholic from the immediate crisis he or she has created, thus relieving the unbearable tension that the Enabler feels because of the situation. In reality, the Enabler is relieving his or her own anxiety rather than giving the alcoholic constructive help. Sometimes the Enabler is someone from outside the family, but more frequently, this role is played by a significant other, a well-meaning or concerned parent, or another close family member.

Professionally, this role is played by ministers, physicians, lawyers, social workers, and other members of the helping professions. If these professionals have not been instructed in the nature and progression of the illness of alcoholism, they may react to the crisis in the same manner as a concerned parent or friend. This anxious rescuing of alcoholics denies them the process of learning and maturing through assuming responsibility for their own behavior and their own messes. It also conditions them to assume that there will always be a protector who will come to their rescue, and in spite of the fact that Enablers insist after each repeated crisis that they will never again rescue the alcoholic, they always do. Rescue operations are performed as compulsively as drinking.

The Victim

The next character to appear on stage is called the Victim. This is the employer, the supervisor, the school principal, a business partner, or a key employee. The Victim assumes responsibility for getting the work done if the alcoholic is absent or unable to perform adequately because of drinking or a hangover. By the time the illness begins to interfere with employment, the alcoholic may have been valuable to the business for ten or fifteen years, and the relationship between the alcoholic and the supervisor may have become a very close one. Protection of the employee by a supervisor is a normal condition, and for the employer or supervisor, there is usually an ongoing hope that the present mistake or absence will be the last one. But it never is.

Yet as the illness of alcoholism progresses, the supervisor's overprotection becomes a key element in the alcoholic's continued problem drinking. The Victim, in effect, tries to save the job and take care of the dependent children for the drinker, just as the Enabler tries to save the alcoholic from the crisis. We become aware in viewing this scene that this employment problem is repeated over and over again by both parties.

The Provoker

The third character in this act is a key person in the play: the partner or parent in the life of the alcoholic. These people are veterans at this role, since they have played it much longer than the other characters in the drama. They are provoked by the recurrent drinking episodes, but they hold the family together despite alcoholism's disrupting factors. In turn, they become the source of provocation. They control, coerce, and adjust. They never give up, never give in, never let go, and never forget. The attitudes of alcoholics often allow for their own failures, but the Provokers in their lives must never fail them. They will declare their freedom to do as they please, but the Provoker, especially if this person is a partner, must do as the alcoholic instructs—must be at home when the alcoholic arrives, *if* he or she arrives.

Another name for this character might be the Compensator, for this person constantly adjusts to every crisis produced by the drinker, compensating for everything that goes wrong within the home and within the relationship. This role may also be played by a child, most often the alcoholic's oldest son or daughter. This child assumes responsibility for resolving the crises, keeping the peace, protecting the other children, and providing appropriate care for the whole family. It is as if the child who is the Compensator reverses roles with the parent and, in attitude and behavior, becomes a "parent" to the parent.

The Compensator, in addition to being partner, parent, or child, frequently plays the additional roles of nurse, physician, and counselor in a dedicated effort to hold the home together. If the Compensator is the partner of an alcoholic, he or she may take on another role—that of primary or sole breadwinner. Compensators attempt to be all things to all people, and by attempting to do so, they may bring injury to themselves and all involved. And no matter what the alcoholic does or does not do, when the crisis has subsided, the alcoholic ends up "at home," for this is where we all go when there is no other place to go.

Act 2 is now played out in full. The alcoholic is no longer helpless, having been rescued, put back to work, restored as a member of the family, and reclothed in the costume of a responsible adult. The rescue, however, has increased the alcoholic's dependency and denial, because the consequences of drinking were removed by others and the entire mess cleared up by people other than the one who made it. People other than the drinker suffered the consequences of his or her drinking, which permitted the alcoholic to use drinking as a very convenient problem-solving device. Drinking removed the psychic pain, and the characters in act 2 removed the painful consequences of the drinking episode.

ACT 3

Act 3 begins in much the same fashion as act 1, but a new dimension has been added. The alcoholic's need for denial is now greater, and he or she is now uncomfortably dependent. The denial becomes louder and stronger. The alcoholic denies having a drinking problem and that drinking has caused any trouble. The alcoholic denies that anyone really helped, denies that the job is in jeopardy, and insists that he or she is the best person in the workplace. Alcoholics blame the family for all the fuss, nagging, and trouble that developed—often insisting that the partner is crazy and needs to see a psychiatrist. In some instances, as the hostility in the relationship intensifies, the alcoholic may hurl unwarranted accusations of infidelity at the partner, knowing they are not true.

Alcoholics are painfully aware of the truth they so vocally deny. They are aware of their drunkenness and the resulting failures. Their guilt and remorse are overwhelming, and the memory of their dependence on others becomes almost unbearable.

There are some drinkers who achieve the same sort of denial through stony silence and refusal to discuss anything related to the drinking episode—the memory is too painful. Some insist or even demand that the family remain silent on the subject. Other drinkers may insist that family members admit their own mistakes in responding to the drinking episode, reversing the drinker's responsibility. When this occurs, it is never forgotten, by either the alcoholic or the family members who participated.

Within a reasonable period of time, the family adjusts to whatever is the norm. The alcoholic member denies that he or she will ever drink again, and the other cast members give similar promises: The Enabler will never again come to the rescue, the Victim will not tolerate another drinking episode, and the Provoker assures the alcoholic partner that he or she cannot continue to live under these conditions.

The entire dialogue consists of denial on the part of all actors, since it is in stark contrast to reality. The Enabler, the Victim, and the Provoker have all made promises before and failed to follow through. The end results are increased anxiety and resentment for all involved and an open invitation for the alcoholic to again exercise his or her sense of superiority. If this occurs, the alcoholic's reservoir of tension, loneliness, and guilt becomes unbearable, and there is only one certain means of relief from the pain: The alcoholic will drink again.

When the alcoholic begins drinking, the play does not come to an end. Audience members may feel they are watching a three-part movie rather than a play, for the play has suddenly returned to act 1 without the curtain coming down. If the audience remains seated long enough, all three acts will be played out again identically; at the end of act 3, the alcoholic will drink again. The play continues to run year after year. The characters get older, but there is little, if any, change in the script or the action.

If the first two acts are played out as described earlier, act 3 will follow in similar fashion. If act 1 did not occur, we would not have the beginning of the play *Alcoholism: A Merry-Go-Round Named Denial*, and the drama surrounding it would not exist. This leaves act 2 as the only act in which the tragic drama of alcoholism can be changed or, in terms of achieving earlier sobriety for the alcoholic, the only act in which recovery can be initiated by someone other than the alcoholic. The key to this situation lies in the fact that in act 2 the alcoholic is the recipient of the action, not the initiator. Only in this act is there real potential to break the tragic cycle of denial.

RECOVERY BEGINS IN ACT 2

If recovery from active alcoholism is to begin, it will start with the characters in the second act, who can learn to recognize the dynamics of the illness and to think and behave in a realistic, responsible, and consistent fashion. If act 2 is rewritten and replayed with each character behaving realistically and responsibly, there is every reason to anticipate that all cast members, including the alcoholic, will recover. Since the drinker is locked into a phase of resistance to change, the other actors in act 2 hold the key to the alcoholic's ability to unlock the phase. Alcoholics cannot keep the merry-go-round going unless others ride it with them and help keep it going. It is unreasonable to assume that alcoholics cannot be helped until they want help; it is reasonable to assume that most alcoholics will continue drinking as long as others do for them what they should do for themselves.

It is important to realize that the three supporting actors in the drama did not learn to play their respective roles overnight. They play the roles that they perceive to be expected of them. They sincerely believe they are helping the drinker and do not understand that they are helping to perpetuate the drinking.

Enablers believe that it is wrong to let alcoholics suffer the consequences of their drinking when suffering can be prevented so easily by a simple rescue operation. They see it as similar to saving a drowning person: It simply must be done. But the rescue mission also relieves the anxiety of the Enabler and conveys to the alcoholic the negative message "You cannot make it without my help." The Enabler's well-meaning action may indicate a lack of confidence in the alcoholic's ability to be responsible for himself or herself.

Provokers are subverted in most of their attempts to cope with the drinking situation. If they are partners, they can become exhausted by the almost constant barrage of hostility the drinker directs toward them, and they almost inevitably feed back into the relationship their own bitterness, anger, and anxiety. If they take legal action or effect a separation, they are often treated by the other cast members as if they were deserting the play.

If there are children in the home, the Provoker can seek professional help in order to lessen his or her own anxiety and thereby prevent involving the children in any intervention with the drinker. However, the partner who continues to play the role of Provoker "for the sake of the children" is hurting rather than helping them.

PROFESSIONAL ENABLERS

Today there are many well-informed professionals who work effectively with alcoholics and their families, but there are also many professionals who unwittingly play the role of professional Enablers. They all too often encourage or assist the family in defusing the immediate crisis rather than encouraging the members to calm down, back off a bit, and give the drinker the time—and the responsibility—to resolve his or her own crisis. Sometimes professional Enablers, in their own anxious efforts to be of help, usurp the family's responsibility by becoming the key player in act 2. They enter into the family interaction and take charge. Family members assume that the professional knows best, and in their search for someone to lead, they encourage the professional to take charge. Although this type of trust may be flattering to the professional, it hinders the corrective process. Rather than learning to rely on their own judgment, members of the family may pressure the professional to tell them what to do and when to do it. The professional may then unconsciously take on the role of Enabler and rescue the alcoholic's family by coercing the alcoholic into treatment of one type or another. And the merry-go-round continues. Regardless of who rescues whom, a rescue mission is a rescue mission.

Family members, including the alcoholic, must be given the time, the freedom, and the dignity to make their own decisions and set their own directions. The professional's primary role is to help these families reduce their level of anxiety. This is done most effectively by the professional who is able to stay outside the field of anxiety, think clearly, and maintain an interested and objective view of everyone involved.

Dr. Dan Papero of the Georgetown Family Center in Washington, D.C., has stated the following: "If the professional interprets what he or she hears from the family as being traumatic, the family will be traumatized." If the professional understands the nature of the illness and is knowledgeable about the predictable behavior characteristics of the drinker and the family, he or she can greatly help all involved by remaining attentive, objective, and calm. The role of professionals is first to educate themselves about the nature of alcoholism, then to educate those who ask for help. Education in this sense also includes knowledge about other services available that might provide help for the drinker and the family.

All families, regardless of social status, education, race, financial status, or religious creed—or lack of it—know best what to do for themselves. They can both verbalize and act on this knowledge if their anxiety is reduced sufficiently.

THE MORAL ISSUE

The moral issue is important: No one has the right to play God and demand that the alcoholic stop drinking. The reverse is also true: The alcoholic does not have the right to make unreasonable demands of family and friends. And since family and friends are assumed to be sober and more clearheaded than the alcoholic, they must learn to think and act in freedom from the alcoholic's dominance. For some, this stage may occur within weeks, but for others, especially if they have played the role of Provoker, it may take months or even years. Two factors all too often abort a recovery program for the Provoker: The alcoholic's response may move from disapproval to direct threats of violence to himself or herself or to others, or the Provoker may be so overloaded with family and employment responsibilities that he or she will find regular attendance in a recovery program difficult.

There is no easy way to stop the merry-go-round. To spell out concise rules that apply to all members of the cast, or to any one role, is impossible, since all situations are different. And often cast members are able to see the alcoholic's merry-go-round, but they fail to comprehend that they provide the resources that help to keep it going. The thing that keeps them so emotionally blind is the underlying fear that their alcoholic loved one won't make it without their help. Ironically, it is this very type of help that permits the drinker to continue to ride the merry-go-round.

If family and friends continue to ride the merry-go-round with the alcoholic year after year, the following situations will likely occur:

1. Excessive drinking and other related illnesses will shorten the alcoholic's life considerably. Alcoholics sometimes hit bottom in their later years when the excessive drinking has resulted in serious physical and emotional impairment.
2. The alcoholic may eventually hit bottom and quit drinking, but as long as others continue their overinvestment in the alcoholic's life, the chance of early cessation of drinking is very slim.
3. If family and friends do not change, the alcoholic (whether sober or drinking) will find some method of distancing from this overinvestment in his or her life. Methods of distancing include (a) overinvolvement in work or special interests, (b) overinvolvement in recovery groups and with individual members, and (c) involvement in sexual relationships with

people other than the existing partner. An alcoholic may quit drinking yet have the same difficult relationship problems. Cessation of drinking is one thing; sobriety is another.

4. If, because of pressure from outside the home, the alcoholic person gets off the merry-go-round while the family still rides, the family will automatically shift its anxious concerns to another family member, and the drama will keep going with a new star, front and center.

5. The family and friends, in focusing their attention on the alcoholic, will ignore their own wants and needs.

ALCOHOLIC SONS AND DAUGHTERS

If the alcoholic is a young person who is still living at home with one or both parents, the situation is much the same as that of the older alcoholic. But here the intense interaction is played out between parents, or parental figures, and the children, both the alcoholic child or other children in the family, which sets the stage for the older alcoholic's relationship process. Quite early, alcoholic offspring become the focus of anxiety and overinvestment on the part of one or both parents. If this is a son, he may have a very close relationship with his mother, who appears to place more importance on her relationship with him than on the one with her partner. In some cases, her partner has a drinking problem, or he may have deserted the family. If he hasn't deserted them physically, he may have deserted them emotionally in his own efforts to cope. The mother then shifts her energy into the lives of one or more of her children, most often a son, who she hopes will in some way compensate for her distant or absent partner. In time, the son will attempt to declare his independence from this intense relationship but may be fearful of trying to make it on his own, so he becomes ambivalent, declaring his independence one day and asking for her protection the next. If alcohol or other drugs provide him with a false sense of well-being and temporary relief, he may be dependent on chemicals by the time he's a senior in high school.

As an adult, he usually selects a partner with a level of emotional intensity equal to his mother's, and the ambivalence continues.

If the young alcoholic is a daughter, it's basically the same type of situation except that the overinvestment is provided more often by the father or father figure. Very early in her life, the daughter and her mother may develop an uncomfortable or even negative relationship. The mother may be overly critical of her daughter or preoccupied with other difficulties outside this relationship. The daughter then shifts her original attachment away from her mother and onto her father, who reciprocates. The relationship between daughter and father often develops into an intense and overly close one. As the daughter grows up, she may find it difficult to become independent of the father, his assistance, and his protection. On the other hand, she will likely want a life of her own and sincerely try to relieve her parents of their responsibility for her. She may become ambivalent and insecure, moving toward the father in a dependent fashion, then moving away, declaring her ability to make it completely on her own. As with her male counterpart, if she finds that alcohol or other drugs provide her with a temporary sense of well-being, autonomy, and independence, she may develop another dependency—on alcohol or other drugs—by the time she is ready to leave home for her first real job or college.

Both these young alcoholics will most often tend to relive the original family interaction in their choice of mates. The son will find a partner who overinvests in him both emotionally and physically. This relationship becomes a push-pull or close-distant interaction, and the two begin riding the merry-go-round very early in the relationship.

The daughter usually finds a partner who she thinks will protect her from life's pain. When the partner can no longer deal with her idealistic expectations, the partner will back off, which she, in turn, is likely to interpret as abandonment or rejection. Out of concern for her helplessness and the partner's own strong sense of guilt, the partner tries to fulfill the role she expects; in this situation, both parties often end up with a drinking problem. They, too, board the merry-go-round very early in the relationship.

In these two examples, the parents unknowingly play the roles of both Enablers and Provokers; consequently, it is the responsibility of any professionals who become involved in such situations to work with the parents of these young people.

THE ALCOHOLIC HOMEMAKER OR UNEMPLOYED PERSON

For those who wish to structure the merry-go-round for the alcoholic who is a homemaker or unemployed, the process is quite simple. The spouses in this drama play all three major roles in the second act. If they expect their alcoholic spouses to recover, they must change all three of their roles, and to do this, they need more help than the spouse of an employed alcoholic does. These three-role spouses will deny that they need help, but that is, after all, the name of the play: *A Merry-Go-Round Named Denial*.

THE SENIOR ALCOHOLIC

As baby boomers reach retirement, there are indications that alcoholism is on the increase for this demographic. The roles played by the supporting cast may apply more to sons, daughters, and well-meaning friends than to spouses and employers, but the basic message of the play is the same: Role changes must occur in act 2. The number of elderly persons who misuse or abuse illicit drugs and alcohol may continue to increase because baby boomers have higher rates of use of these substances than previous generations.

INITIATING RECOVERY

If a friend is called on for help, he or she should consider it an opportunity to lead the alcoholic and the family into a structured program of recovery.

If someone *thinks* his or her partner has a drinking problem or repeatedly drinks too much, he or she should seek competent help and counsel for the purpose of evaluation. If the person *knows* that a partner has a drinking problem, he or she should seek counsel with the intent of entering an education program as well as individual therapy. These sessions should not be abandoned after a few visits, for changes do not occur overnight. Regular weekly attendance is important, and many partners and other family members report that it takes at least six months to begin gaining realistic benefits from group participation or individual therapy.

If the alcoholic's significant other is a parent, these suggestions also apply. Unfortunately, older parents of alcoholics tend to have more difficulty accepting the painful realities of this illness and their own destructive but well-meaning roles in its perpetuation. They need encouragement from friends and family to continue seeking help after they first reach out for it.

Although professional help is valuable and plays an important role in the recovery process, it is not always available or affordable for the alcoholic and family. Alcoholics Anonymous (AA) is the most widespread self-help group for the alcoholic today. It is the most readily available program for the drinker, and its track record for success is without equal. If other treatment is available for the drinker, AA is often recommended during and after treatment. It is important to know, however, that there are people who prefer other ways of maintaining sobriety and that their methods and opinions are respected.

Al-Anon, a program parallel to AA, is the most readily available help for family members, friends, and significant others of alcoholics. Like AA, it is an ongoing self-help group, and its track record for helping family and friends learn how to develop and maintain their own sense of self-worth and serenity is unmatched. As with AA, Al-Anon is not everyone's preference. Other ways are respected.

In most communities today, there are alcoholism information centers, inpatient and outpatient treatment centers, and mental health centers available, and many private agencies and therapists can provide competent help for alcoholics and their families. Where these services are not available, AA and Al-Anon and other self-help groups usually are. Once family members enter a recovery program, they will benefit if they stick with it in spite of the possibility that recovery may cause greater conflict and suffering at the outset. In the long run, it is far less painful than going round and round and up and down on the merry-go-round of denial.

GUIDELINES FOR THE FAMILY

1. Remove the emotional focus from the alcoholic member. Make every effort to assume responsibility for your own part in this regressive process.
2. Educate yourself about alcoholism.
3. Seek out professional alcoholism services in your own community. Use whatever is available for the family, and know what is available for the alcoholic.
4. Attend Al-Anon or other professional services regularly. If Al-Anon is not available, attend open meetings of Alcoholics Anonymous or other groups appropriate for you.
5. Remember that all human beings and all living things are dependent. Dependence itself is not a pathology, but having too much or too little of it can become pathological.
6. Avoid getting caught up in terms and issues that provoke unnecessary anxiety. Get on with your life.
7. Please keep in mind that not all alcoholics, family members, and friends of alcoholics fit the personalities and characteristics described in this pamphlet. Alcoholics—and the rest of us—possess a variety of personalities and human characteristics. The bottom line is that we are all human beings who try in our own individual ways to make life worthwhile, and in the long run, we are all more alike than we are different.